30 minute French meals made simple

Exclusive to Howdens Joinery Co.

HOWDENS

JOINERY CO.

MAKING SPACE MORE VALUABLE

Valerie Berry

30 minute French meals made simple

With busy lives, we're all looking for quicker ways to help us make delicious meals. This book is designed to help you do just that – with dishes that will impress your friends and family.

I've chosen classic French recipes that are simple to prepare. You'll see how to cook them to perfection, quickly and easily – whether you're an experienced cook or just starting to learn. They're all designed to take no more than 30 minutes, so whether you're making a midweek family meal or a three-course dinner, you'll find a great choice of tasty, time-saving ideas.

All the recipes have been cooked using Lamona appliances, so I know you can produce beautiful results. Cooking is about more than following a recipe. The comfort of your kitchen and the reliability of your equipment are what make you a confident cook.

I hope this book will inspire you to explore the delights of French cooking.

Valerie Berry

Food Stylist and Writer

The French Kitchen

Food is very important in French culture, and whether entertaining friends or relaxing with the family, the kitchen plays a central role. So a French-inspired kitchen has that spirit of generosity and warmth, with a large dining table, clever ingredient storage and places to display prized utensils, pans and crockery.

Our French Connection

This book of French recipes is a special one for Howdens, as we also have a business in France called Houdan Cuisines.

Set up in 2005, Houdan Cuisines shares Howdens' commitment to supplying well-designed, good quality kitchens and appliances from local stock to professional fitters and builders who will install them in your home.

The French are rightly proud of their cooking – which includes not only the classics of haute cuisine but also a wide range of regional French dishes that have become famous around the world.

French culinary traditions are deep-rooted, and even today everyday life in France is marked by three traditional meals. For the French, eating is a ritual and the idea of sharing is an essential part of it. Meals are a pleasure to be shared with family and friends. This book will show you how easy it is to achieve the authentic taste of France in your own Howdens kitchen.

Originally established in the Paris region and the north of France, Houdan Cuisines now has 11 depots, with more set to open in 2015.

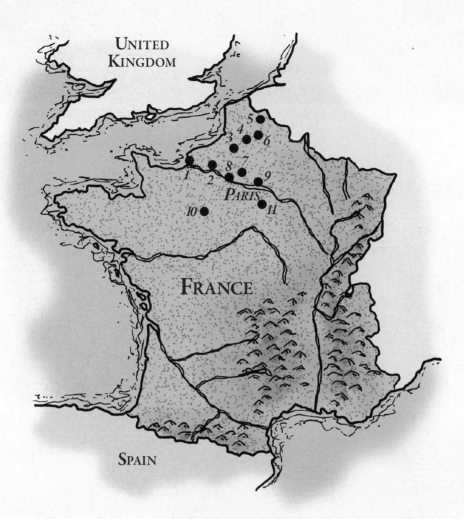

Our Houdan Cuisines Depots

1 Le Havre
2 Rouen
3 Amiens
4 Arras
5 Lille
6 Douai

7 Argenteuil
8 Bezons
9 Aubervilliers
10 Chartres
11 Vitry Sur Seine

(v) = vegetarian

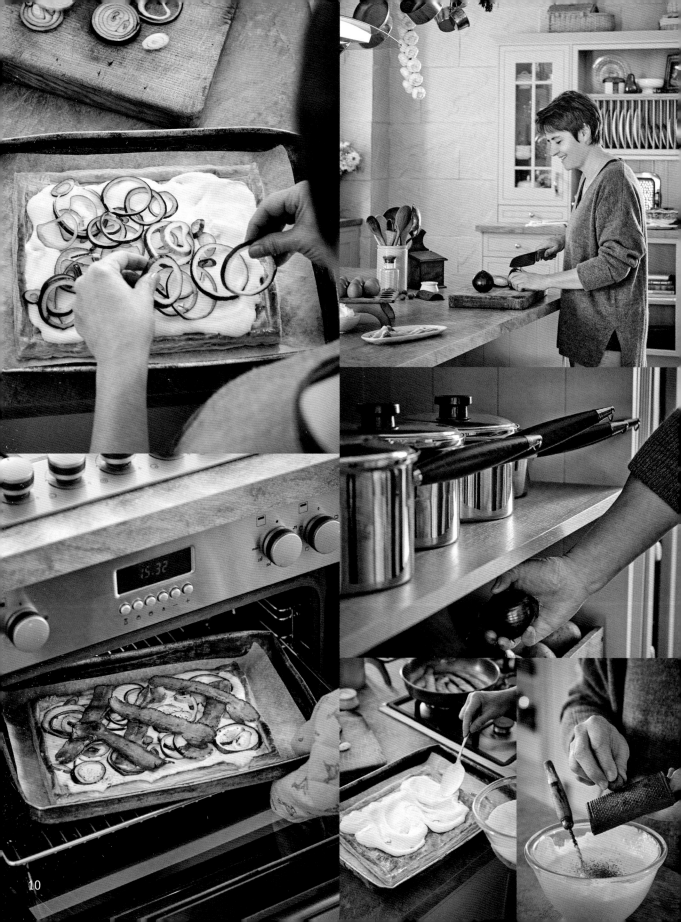

Les entrées / Starters

Discover the secrets of a perfect poached egg – and learn how to enhance the taste of tomatoes, whip up a Hollandaise sauce, and impress your friends with authentic French bistro flavours. As well as using these recipes as delicious starters for an evening meal, you can also enjoy them as light lunches or tasty snacks at any time of day.

Serves 4
10 mins preparation
10 mins cooking

Asperges Sauce Hollandaise

Asparagus with Hollandaise Sauce

Ingredients

24 large green asparagus
200g butter
3 medium egg yolks, lightly beaten
Juice and grated zest of 1 lemon
Sea salt and milled black pepper

To serve
Crusty bread

Equipment
Electric hand mixer

Hollandaise is the mother of all butter sauces. You can make it in a blender, but I find it easier on the stove with an electric hand mixer – and this gives you a lighter texture. In France, we always eat asparagus with our fingers, never with a knife and fork. But I'll leave that up to you!

1. Wash and trim the asparagus and keep to one side.

2. Cut the butter into chunks. Keep 5g to one side, and place the rest in a medium-size saucepan. Warm over a low heat for 5 minutes, until the butter has melted, but not boiling. Remove the whitish froth that floats to the top, and transfer the melted butter to a jug (it will be easier to pour later).

3. In the same saucepan, mix the eggs, 1 tablespoon of lemon juice, 2 tablespoons of water, a good pinch of salt and 5 turns of the peppermill. Place on a very low heat and whisk with an electric hand mixer at low speed. After about 1½ minutes, the mixture should be frothy and thickened, but be careful not to let the eggs become scrambled.

4. Gradually whisk in the warm butter – very slowly at the beginning, then more rapidly when the sauce starts to thicken. Stop adding the butter when you get to the white residue at the bottom of the jug. Check the seasoning and keep the sauce to one side while you cook the asparagus.

5. Place the asparagus in a large frying pan and cover with boiling water from the kettle. Bring to a simmer and cook for 2-3 minutes – they should still have a bite.

6. Drain the asparagus and add the 5g of butter you saved, along with the lemon zest. Season with more salt and pepper, and toss.

7. Divide the asparagus between 4 plates and let your guests help themselves to the Hollandaise.

Try serving this with... a white Côtes de Provence or a white Côtes de Rhone.

Frisée aux Lardons et Oeuf Poché

Curly Endive Salad with Bacon, Poached Egg and Croutons

Ingredients

1 small shallot
100g unsmoked bacon rashers
80g baguette
2 tablespoons red wine vinegar
Sea salt and milled black pepper
4 tablespoons groundnut or grapeseed oil
2 tablespoons Dijon mustard
30g butter, melted
4 large eggs
200g curly endive or mixed lettuce with curly endive

The secret of making a well-formed poached egg is ensuring it's very fresh – as an egg ages, the white tends to leave fine strands in the water. If you're not sure how fresh your eggs are, this foolproof recipe uses cling film to keep everything in shape. The rest of the salad is delicious too!

1. Bring a saucepan of water to a simmer.

2. Finely chop the shallot, and cut the bacon into 4cm chunks. Cut the baguette into 2cm cubes.

3. Make a vinaigrette by mixing the shallot, red wine vinegar, salt and pepper in a bowl. Slowly whisk in the oil, starting with half a teaspoon at a time. When all the oil is incorporated, whisk in the mustard. The vinaigrette should be thick but fluid. This is the basic French vinaigrette – good with any salad. Keep to one side.

4. Cook the bacon in a frying pan over a medium heat for 2 minutes. Add the baguette cubes and cook for another 3 minutes, stirring occasionally, until you have crisp, golden croutons. Remove from the heat and keep covered.

5. Line a small bowl or a teacup with a 35cm square of cling film, and brush lightly with melted butter. Crack an egg in the centre. Gather the sides of the cling film, letting out all the air, and twist tightly. Repeat with the other eggs. Drop the cling-filmed eggs in the simmering water and cook for 6 minutes. Remove and keep to one side.

6. Mix the leaves and vinaigrette. Divide the salad between 4 plates and arrange the bacon and croutons on top. Carefully unwrap the eggs and place one on top of each salad.

Lovely with... a red from the Loire Valley, such as a Saumur-Champigny.

La Salade de Tomates du Midi

Provençal Tomato Salad

Ingredients

5 medium ripe tomatoes
½ teaspoon sea salt
1 small garlic clove
¼ teaspoon sugar
2 teaspoons red wine vinegar
4 tablespoons extra virgin olive oil
5 basil leaves, torn roughly
Milled black pepper

To serve

Crusty baguette

I used to think there was no need for a tomato salad recipe. Then, one day, while buying tomatoes in a market in Nice, a charming old lady spent a good 20 minutes explaining how to make a proper tomato salad. I've followed her advice ever since – and here's her recipe, which is easy to scale up to serve 4.

1. Core and thinly slice the tomatoes. Arrange them overlapping on a serving dish and sprinkle evenly with ½ teaspoon of salt. Leave for 10 minutes – this will remove some of the watery juices and concentrate the taste.

2. Meanwhile, halve the garlic and remove the bitter green centre (if there is one). Crush the garlic into a small bowl.

3. Add the sugar and mix with the back of a wooden spoon until well blended, and almost like a mousse. Add the vinegar and mix until well combined. Slowly whisk in the olive oil, drop by drop at the beginning, then more rapidly, until well blended.

4. Place a sheet of kitchen paper on the tomatoes to absorb the salt and juice. Then, holding the tomatoes in place with the paper, tip the dish to drain off most of the tomato water. Discard the wet paper.

5. Drizzle the dressing over the tomatoes, sprinkle with the torn basil leaves and a grind of black pepper. Serve with a good crusty baguette.

And to drink... a rosé from Provence; if possible, one from Bellet in the Nice area.

Parfait de Foies de Volaille aux Noix

Chicken Liver and Walnut Parfait

Ingredients

450g chicken livers, firm and pale pink rather than dark red
30g butter, plus 100g for the top
2 tablespoons Cognac or whisky
1 shallot, finely chopped
50g walnuts
½ baguette, thinly sliced
5 tablespoons crème fraîche, well chilled
1 pinch cayenne pepper
Sea salt and milled black pepper
4 teaspoons fresh chives, chopped

Equipment
Food processor
4 ramekin dishes

This is a very quick, simple way to make a light, creamy chicken liver parfait. You can serve it with my even quicker 'instant fig chutney': simply process ten ready-to-eat dried figs with a tablespoon of port and a tablespoon of red wine vinegar.

1. Pre-heat the grill to maximum.

2. Trim the chicken livers, discarding any stringy, white, greenish or bloody bits. Poke all over with the tip of a knife to prevent them from spattering too much when cooking.

3. Fry the chicken livers in 15g of butter, over a high heat for 3 minutes, until well charred but still pink inside.

4. Add the Cognac or whisky and let it boil down completely, which will take about 30-60 seconds. Transfer to a plate and leave to cool for 5 minutes.

5. In the same frying pan, fry the shallot and walnuts in 15g of butter for 5 minutes. Transfer to the food processor and leave to cool.

6. Meanwhile, spread the baguette slices on a grill pan or oven tray with a wire rack. Toast under the grill for 1½-2 minutes on each side.

7. Process the shallot and walnuts until the walnuts are reduced to a powder. Add the chicken livers, crème fraîche, cayenne pepper and seasoning, and whiz until well blended.

8. Check the seasoning and divide between the 4 ramekins. Sprinkle the chives over the top and serve straight away – or cover with a thin layer of butter and keep in the fridge until you're ready to serve.

Tip: This parfait will keep in the fridge for 4 days.

Perfect with... a semi-dry white from the Loire valley, like a Vouvray; or you could serve it with a Dubonnet Faux Martini (see page 98 for my recipe).

Tartare de Saumon et Concombre Marinés

Cured Salmon and Cucumber Tartare

Ingredients

300g salmon fillet, skin removed
½ teaspoon sea salt
½ teaspoon sugar
Juice and grated zest of 1 lemon
1 large cucumber
1 teaspoon Dijon mustard
2 tablespoons fromage frais
2 tablespoons fresh dill, chopped
Sea salt and milled black pepper

To serve
Fresh dill
Salad leaves

These days, 'tartare' means anything finely chopped, usually raw, and dressed in a sauce or seasoned. In this refreshing summer starter, the salmon is lightly cured with salt and lemon, and combined with a subtle mustard dressing.

1. Cut the salmon into very small cubes and place in a bowl. Add the salt, sugar, lemon juice and zest, and toss until the salmon is well coated. Leave for 10 minutes.

2. Using a vegetable peeler, cut 16 long strips off the cucumber, turning it when you reach the seeded centre. Finely chop 8 of the strips and keep the rest for garnish.

3. Drain any moisture from the marinated salmon. Add the chopped cucumber, mustard, fromage frais and fresh dill. Mix together and check the seasoning.

4. Divide the mixture between 4 serving plates, spooning it into the centre. Wrap 2 cucumber strips around each serving of the salmon tartare. Garnish with fresh dill and salad leaves.

Goes very nicely with... a glass of Champagne or a white Burgundy like a Petit Chablis.

Oeuf Cocotte à l'Estragon

Baked Eggs with Tarragon

Ingredients

15g butter, melted
4 medium eggs
2 tablespoons fresh tarragon, chopped
2 tablespoons crème fraîche
Sea salt and milled black pepper
2 slices rye sourdough bread,
toasted, buttered and cut into strips

Equipment

2 ramekin dishes (150ml)

Oeuf cocotte are eggs baked in a ramekin, traditionally in a 'bain-marie' (water bath). But this is a much easier way to get a nice set white and runny yolk – perfect for a romantic breakfast treat.

1. Pre-heat the oven to 200°C/fan 180°C/gas mark 6.

2. Brush the inside of each ramekin with melted butter.

3. Crack 2 eggs over each ramekin, letting the white fall and keeping the yolks in the shell, being careful not to break them. Place the half shells with the yolks back in the egg box for later.

4. Place the ramekins on a small baking tray and bake for 10 minutes. Remove from the oven, and sprinkle each one with a tablespoon of tarragon. Top each ramekin with 2 of the reserved egg yolks and a tablespoon of crème fraîche. Season well.

5. Return the ramekins to the oven and bake for a further 7 minutes. Serve them straight out of the oven with 'mouillettes', the French version of soldiers. Be careful, the ramekins will be hot!

Tip: You can add anything you fancy with the egg yolks and crème fraîche – such as smoked salmon, cooked spinach, cooked mushrooms or grated cheese.

To drink... a glass of Mimosa (see page 96 for my recipe).

Tarte Façon Flammekueche

Onion, Bacon and Cream Tart

Ingredients

3 medium egg yolks
2 pinches sea salt
320g pack ready rolled all
butter puff pastry
1 red onion
100g smoked streaky bacon
150g fromage frais
150g crème fraîche
¼ teaspoon nutmeg, freshly grated
Milled black pepper

To serve

Green salad

Equipment

Baking parchment

This Alsatian cousin of the pizza was made traditionally from scraps of bread to test the heat of the wood-fired oven while waiting for the main loaf to prove. My version is equally delicious, using a puff pastry base. Make sure you buy a good quality French crème fraîche, preferably d'Isigny, which gives a lovely smooth texture when it cooks.

1. Pre-heat the oven to 200°C/fan 180°C/gas mark 6. Line the oven tray with baking parchment.

2. Mix the three egg yolks with a large pinch of salt.

3. Unroll the pastry, prick with a folk and place on the prepared oven tray. Using the tip of a knife, mark a line around the pastry, 1 centimetre inside the edge. Lightly brush with some of the salted egg yolk mixture, place in the oven on the lowest shelf and bake for 10 minutes.

4. Meanwhile, finely slice the onion, and fry the bacon in a large frying pan over a high heat for 2 minutes. Mix the fromage frais, crème fraîche, egg yolks and nutmeg with a large pinch of salt and around 10 turns of the peppermill, to suit your taste.

5. Remove the puff pastry from the oven and turn up the temperature to 220°C/fan 200°C/gas mark 7.

6. Press the centre of the pastry, inside the knife markings, with the back of a spoon to create a contained space for the topping. Spread the fromage frais mixture over the recessed surface. Arrange the sliced onion on top, then the cooked bacon.

7. Bake for 10 minutes on the lowest shelf, until the topping is set and the bacon is crisp. Cut into 4 and serve with a salad.

   Tip: For best result and a crispier base, use the conventional oven setting.

This recipes calls for... a Pinot Noir from Alsace.

Champignons Beurre à l'Ail

Baked Mushrooms with Garlic Butter

Ingredients

12 medium chestnut mushrooms
100g butter at room temperature
20g shallots, roughly chopped
2 large garlic cloves, crushed
20g fresh parsley, roughly chopped
¼ teaspoon nutmeg, freshly grated
¼ teaspoon sea salt
15g ground almonds
Milled black pepper

To serve

Crusty baguette

Equipment

Food processor (optional)
12-hole muffin tin

If you love mushrooms, this is the perfect way to eat them – and because of the garlic your kitchen will smell just like a French bistro! Make sure you have plenty of crusty bread to mop up the buttery juices.

1. Pre-heat the oven to 200°C/fan 180°C/gas mark 6. Place a baking tray on the lowest shelf.

2. Clean the mushrooms – but don't use running water, as mushrooms absorb it like sponges. Instead, wipe any dirt away with slightly damp kitchen paper.

3. Trim off the stems, right down to the base. (You could keep the stems, and use them chopped and fried in a variation of the Oeuf Cocotte, see page 22 for my recipe.)

4. Place the butter, shallots, garlic, parsley, nutmeg, salt, almonds and 10 grinds of the peppermill in a food processor. Process until well blended. Alternatively, chop the shallots, garlic and parsley very finely and incorporate into the butter along with the nutmeg, salt and almonds.

5. Fill each mushroom cap with a heaped tablespoon of the garlic butter and place in the muffin tin. Put the tin on the hot baking tray and cook for 15 minutes until the butter bubbles.

6. Spoon the mushrooms and butter juices onto 2 plates, and serve with a crusty baguette.

   Tip: I use a muffin tin rather than a flat tray so the melting butter bastes the mushrooms instead of spreading out.

Try these with... a red Sancerre from the Nivernais or Red Givry from Burgundy.

Les plats / Main courses

When I was growing up in France, classic dishes like steak with Béarnaise sauce were Sunday treats – and mastering sauces was what made you a great cook. Here you'll see how to prepare some of the cornerstones of French cuisine in next to no time. I've also included some easy vegetarian delicacies, like a feathery light soufflé omelette.

Fish

We adore fish and seafood in France – whether it's classics such as moules marinière or more contemporary dishes like baked sea bass. The great thing about fish is it cooks quickly, so these recipes are perfect for midweek family meals as well as dinner parties.

Moules Marinière

Mussels in White Wine Sauce

Serves 4
15 mins preparation
10 mins cooking

Ingredients

2.5kg mussels
60g butter
100g shallots, finely chopped
1 stick celery, finely chopped
3 garlic cloves, finely chopped
50g fresh parsley, chopped
300ml white wine
(preferably Muscadet)
Milled black pepper

To serve

Crusty bread or chips

Equipment

Large 5-litre cooking pot with a lid

The name Marinière comes from the traditional striped shirt worn by Charentais fishermen, designed to make them easy to spot if they fell overboard. This dish has gained iconic status in Lille, where 400 tonnes of mussels are served every year during the two-day 'Grande Braderie'. You can prepare it in lots of ways, but I like the simple approach, with shallots, celery, parsley and white wine.

1. Warm a serving dish and 4 plates in your oven, on its lowest setting.

2. Wash the mussels under cold water, discarding any opened or damaged ones. Remove the 'beards', the seaweed-like strands attached to the side, by pulling them towards the pointed end of the shell.

3. Melt half the butter in the pot. Add the shallots and celery, and cook over a medium heat for 3 minutes, until soft. Add the garlic and half the parsley, and cook for 30 seconds.

4. Add the wine and bring to a boil. Increase the heat to maximum and add the mussels. Cover the pot and cook for 4-5 minutes, stirring occasionally, until all the mussels have opened. Turn off the heat and leave to sit for a couple of minutes.

5. Transfer the mussels to the warm serving dish by spooning them in rather than pouring them out (so the cooking liquid stays in the pot). Keep them warm in the oven.

6. Pass the cooking liquid through a fine sieve to remove any grit or dirt, then pour it into a saucepan and bring to a simmer.

7. Whisk in the rest of the butter and parsley, and add lots of black pepper.

8. Pour the sauce over the mussels and serve at once with crusty bread or chips.

To drink with this... try the same wine as in the recipe: a Muscadet from the North West of the Loire region.

Croustillant de Maquereaux à la Diable

Crusted Mustard, Herb and Breadcrumb Mackerel Fillets

Ingredients

8 mackerel fillets
1 banana shallot, finely chopped
½ teaspoon coriander seeds, crushed
¼ teaspoon milled black pepper
200ml white wine vinegar
50g dried breadcrumbs
20g butter, melted
1 tablespoon fresh chives, chopped
2 tablespoons fresh parsley, chopped
1 tablespoon fresh tarragon, chopped
4 teaspoons Dijon mustard

To serve
Buttered spinach
(see page 68 for my recipe)

Equipment
Baking parchment

As in English, 'à la diable', or devilled, refers to a dish cooked with hot condiments or spices. The mustard in this recipe suits mackerel perfectly, as it cuts the richness of the fish.

1. Pre-heat the oven to 200°C/fan 180°C/gas mark 6. Line a baking tray with baking parchment.

2. Place the mackerel fillets in a glass dish big enough to spread them out in a single layer. Sprinkle with the chopped shallot, coriander seeds and black pepper. Pour the vinegar over the top and leave for 10 minutes while you prepare the rest of the ingredients.

3. Pan-fry the breadcrumbs in the butter for about 2 minutes, until golden and crisp.

4. Dry the mackerel fillets with kitchen paper, reserving the marinade.

5. Pass the vinegar marinade through a sieve. Stir the reserved shallot and spices from the marinade into the breadcrumb mixture, add the chopped chives, parsley and tarragon, and mix well.

6. Place the mackerel fillets on the lined baking tray. Spread ½ teaspoon of mustard evenly over the top of each one, and sprinkle with the breadcrumb mix.

7. Bake for 7-10 minutes, depending on the size of the fillets. Serve hot with buttered spinach.

Enjoy this dish with... a Côtes de Provence Rosé.

Saumon Rôti, Sauce Chèvre et Cresson

Roasted Salmon with Goats' Cheese and Watercress Sauce

Ingredients

4 x 170g salmon fillets with the skins on
1 tablespoon olive oil
Sea salt and milled black pepper
125g soft goats' cheese
125g Greek yogurt
60ml water
60g watercress, finely chopped

To serve
Green beans

Equipment
Electric hand blender or food processor

In France, the famous 'sauce à l'oseille', a sorrel cream sauce, is a traditional accompaniment for salmon. Here, goats' cheese and watercress imitate that sauce to perfection. The French like their salmon crispy on the outside with a creamy centre, which means cooking it slightly 'pink'.

1. Pre-heat the oven to 200°C/fan 180°C/gas mark 6. Line a baking tray with kitchen foil.

2. Heat a large, non-stick frying pan. Brush the salmon fillets with a little oil and season well. Place them in the pan and cook, skin side down, over a medium heat for 2 minutes. Flip them over and cook for 2 more minutes.

3. Transfer the fillets to the baking tray, skin side down, and bake for 8 minutes if you like it slightly pink at the heart, or 10 minutes if you like it more cooked.

4. Meanwhile, mash together the goats' cheese, yogurt and water until smooth. Transfer to a small saucepan and warm gently. Add the watercress, and cook over a low heat for a couple of minutes, until it starts to wilt. Don't let it boil, or the mixture will curdle. Season to taste and leave to infuse.

5. For a smoother texture and a lovely green colour, give it a whiz in the food processor or with an electric hand blender.

6. Place the salmon fillets on plates, drizzle the sauce on top and serve with green beans.

   Tip: Pre-cook the green beans as on page 68, but leave out the butter and reheat them with a hint of olive oil at the last minute.

To drink... a white Sancerre from the South East of the Loire Valley.

Soles Grillées, Façon Meunière, Sauce Câpres et Crevettes Grises

Grilled Dover Sole with Capers and Brown Shrimps

Ingredients

3 tablespoons capers in vinegar
2 tablespoons plain flour
¼ teaspoon milled black pepper
2 x 300g Dover sole (ask the fishmonger to remove the brown skin and scale the white)
80g lightly salted butter, melted
1 banana shallot, finely chopped
80g cooked brown shrimps or tiny prawns, peeled

To serve

1 lemon, halved
Steamed potatoes

Dover sole is a lovely treat, and with this easy, under-the-grill method, you don't have to flip the fish over. The caper and brown shrimp butter is quick to prepare too, at the last minute. If you can't get hold of brown shrimps, you can use small prawns instead.

1. Pre-heat the grill to maximum. Line the oven tray with kitchen foil and place under the grill.

2. Rinse and drain the capers.

3. Mix the flour and black pepper, and spread on a large plate, the size of the fish.

4. Dry the sole with kitchen paper, and dip in the flour until lightly coated on both sides.

5. Take the hot tray from the grill. Brush it carefully with melted butter and lay the fish, white skin side down, on the tray. Drizzle a couple of tablespoons of butter over the top of each sole, slide the tray in the lowest rack and grill for 9 to 10 minutes. You know they're cooked when the flesh comes away easily from the bone.

6. While the fish is cooking, fry the chopped shallot in 2 tablespoons of butter for 2 minutes. Add the capers and fry for 1 more minute, until they puff up.

7. Add the shrimps or prawns, and cook for 30-60 seconds, just to reheat them.

8. Remove the sole from the oven and transfer to 2 plates. Drizzle with the sauce, and serve with lemon halves and steamed potatoes.

This noble fish deserves... a noble white wine, like a Meursault from Burgundy.

Serves 4
15 mins preparation
10 mins cooking

Coquilles St Jacques à la Ventrèche Basque

Bacon-Wrapped Scallops

Ingredients

16 or 20 slices of pancetta
1 teaspoon paprika
1 tablespoon fresh thyme,
finely chopped
16 or 20 scallops, depending
on their size

To serve
Buttered cabbage
(see page 68 for my recipe)

Equipment
Cocktail sticks

The best scallops are sold live in their shells. A good fishmonger will prepare them for you, and you can keep the shells for serving this dish. If you can't buy them live, look for plump scallops with a 'pearly' appearance. 'Ventrèche Basque' is a French version of bacon, rubbed with piment d'Espelette, a type of chilli powder. Here we use pancetta instead, sprinkled lightly with paprika.

1. Lay a slice of pancetta on a chopping board, and stretch it by running the back of a knife along its length. Sprinkle lightly with paprika and thyme, then wrap it around the scallop and secure with a cocktail stick. Repeat until you've wrapped all the scallops.

2. Heat a large non-stick frying pan. Place the wrapped scallops in the pan and cook for 3-4 minutes, depending on their size. Flip them and cook for 3-4 minutes more. Serve 4 or 5 scallops for each person, presented on their shells with buttered cabbage on the side.

Perfect with... a white Burgundy, such as a Chablis.

Bar aux Graines de Fenouil en Croûte de Sel

Baked Sea Bass with Fennel Seeds in a Salt Crust

Ingredients

1.4kg coarse sea salt
100ml water
700g sea bass (this is one whole fish; ask the fishmonger to gut it and remove the gills, but leave the scales on)
2½ teaspoons fennel seeds, crushed

To serve
Extra virgin olive oil
Potato gratin
(see page 64 for my recipe)

Using a salt crust to seal a baked fish is an easy way to trap all the flavours and moisture. It's important to keep the scales on, to prevent the flesh from absorbing the salt. Then you're left with a wonderfully succulent sea bass, which you can enjoy very simply, as they do in the South of France, with a drizzle of olive oil and a sprinkling of fennel seeds.

1. Pre-heat the oven to maximum. Line a baking tray with kitchen foil.

2. Mix the salt and water to form a paste, and spread a third of this on the baking tray in the shape of your fish. Place the fish on top.

3. Rub the cavity of the fish with 2 teaspoons of the crushed fennel seeds. Cover with the rest of the salt paste to enclose the fish completely.

4. Bake in the middle position of the oven for 20 minutes. Remove from the oven, and let the fish rest for 5 minutes.

5. Using the back of a spoon or the point of a knife, carefully break the salt crust and remove it completely from the top of the fish.

6. Remove the skin, lift the fillets and place them on a serving plate. Remove the head and bones and lift the lower fillets onto the serving plate.

7. Serve sprinkled with the remaining ½ teaspoon of fennel seeds and drizzled with extra virgin olive oil. This goes well with a potato gratin.

Tip: Choose a fish that looks 'just-out-of-the-sea' shiny, with bulbous eyes and red gills.

Pair with... a white Bandol from the Provence Alpes Côte d'Azur region.

Les plats / Main courses - Meat

Rich, comforting flavours, served up in style. That's what my meat main courses are all about. In a few simple steps, you can recreate some of my country's truly great dishes – and seriously impress your guests!

Aiguillettes de Poulet Basquaise

Chicken Mini Fillets with Onion, Peppers and Tomato

Ingredients

1 onion, cut into wedges
1 red pepper, deseeded and cut into strips (see tip below)
1 green pepper, deseeded and cut into strips
4 tablespoons olive oil
1 garlic clove, crushed
¼ teaspoon sweet paprika
1 good pinch chilli flakes
400g tinned whole tomatoes, drained and quartered
3 fresh thyme sprigs
1½ tablespoons plain flour
Milled black pepper
¼ teaspoon sea salt
600g chicken mini fillets or chicken breast cut into strips
50g Bayonne or Serrano ham, chopped
200ml white wine

To serve

Sourdough bread
Green salad (see my vinaigrette recipe on page 14)

Equipment

1 plastic freezer bag

This dish from the Basque region is usually prepared with chicken in areas near the mountains, and with tuna along the coast. If you prefer tuna, you can follow the same recipe, but cut the fish into thick strips and reduce the pan-frying time by half.

1. Fry the onion and peppers in half of the olive oil over a high heat for 5 minutes, until slightly caramelised on the edges. Add the garlic, paprika and chilli flakes, and cook for 30 seconds. Add the tomatoes and thyme, reduce the heat to medium and simmer for 15 minutes.

2. Meanwhile, place the flour in a freezer bag, and add about 5 turns of the pepper grinder and the salt. Dry the mini fillets on kitchen paper and add to the bag. Seal the bag and shake to coat the chicken pieces lightly and evenly in flour.

3. In a second frying pan, heat the rest of the oil until hot, add the chicken and fry for 4 minutes. Turn the chicken, add the ham and fry for 5 minutes.

4. Add the wine and let it bubble for 2 minutes, slowly sliding the pan forwards and backwards to distribute the wine evenly and to coat the chicken.

5. Add the chicken pieces and sauce to the onion, pepper and tomato mixture. Stir gently but thoroughly, making sure everything's well combined, then simmer for 3 more minutes.

6. Serve with sourdough bread and a green salad.

Tip: To deseed and slice a pepper quickly, slice off both ends, cut in half lengthways, and run a knife along the inside to remove the central core and seeds. Cut the body and ends into strips.

An appropriate wine... would be a Basque red, like an Irouléguy.

Cuisses de Canard Sauce Bigarade

Duck Legs in Orange Sauce

Ingredients

3 oranges
4 duck legs
Sea salt and milled black pepper
80g granulated sugar
80ml white wine vinegar
2 tablespoons Grand Marnier
or Cointreau (optional)
2 teaspoons good quality
roast chicken gravy mix
300ml ready-made chicken stock

To serve

Petits Pois à la Française
(see page 70 for my recipe)

This classic orange sauce can be traced back to the 1800s, and was originally made with bitter 'bigarade' or Seville oranges. It is still officially called sauce bigarade, but is now made with sweet oranges and vinegar. (Today, bigarade oranges are used mainly to make orange liqueurs.)

1. Pre-heat the oven to 220°C/fan 200°C/gas mark 7. Line the oven tray with kitchen foil.

2. Remove the zest of one orange and juice all the oranges. Heat a large non-stick frying pan. Season the duck legs and place in the hot pan, skin side down. Cook over a high heat for 3 minutes, until golden. Flip over and cook for 2 more minutes.

3. Transfer the duck to the lined oven tray and bake for 20 to 25 minutes, depending on the size.

4. Meanwhile, discard the fat from the frying pan and sprinkle a thin layer of sugar into it. Place over a high heat and cook for 3-4 minutes, until the sugar turns to caramel.

5. Add the vinegar and orange juice – and the Grand Marnier or Cointreau, if you're using them. Be careful, as the liquid may bubble vigorously.

6. Boil down and reduce by half. Don't worry about any pieces of hard caramel; they will dissolve with the boiling.

7. Dissolve the gravy mix in 2 tablespoons of stock, and add this to the orange caramel sauce, along with the rest of the stock and the orange zest. Reduce the heat and simmer for 10 minutes, until thickened.

8. Remove the duck from the oven, transfer to a warm plate and cover with kitchen foil. Leave to rest for 5 minutes.

9. Serve the duck legs drizzled with the sauce and garnished with petits pois.

Tip: Duck breasts are also delicious with this orange sauce. Pan-fry them for 5 minutes as above, and then roast for 10 minutes for medium rare.

To accompany the sweet and sour flavours of the sauce... rich red from the Languedoc-Roussillon.

Côtes de Porc Charcutière

Roasted Pork Chops in Mustard and Gherkin Sauce

Ingredients

1 banana shallot, thinly sliced
30g cured ham, chopped
10g butter
250ml ready-made fresh
chicken stock
1 teaspoon good quality roast
chicken gravy mix
2 pork chops, about 2cm thick
Sea salt and milled black pepper
1 tablespoon mustard
10 gherkins, finely sliced

To serve
Classic French mash
(see page 66 for my recipe)

After the 15th century in France, 'charcutiers' shops, which sold only pork, were allowed to prepare their cuts and sell them cooked – an ancestor of the ready meal! This recipe comes from that tradition, and creates some truly mouth-watering aromas while it's simmering.

1. Pan-fry the shallot and ham with the butter for 3 minutes, until slightly crispy. Add the stock and gravy mix, and simmer for 7 minutes.

2. Taking the pork chops, cut small slits along the fat and season well.

3. Heat a second frying pan on high. When it starts smoking, add the pork chops and reduce the heat to medium. Cook for about 4 minutes on each side, then transfer to a warm plate. Cover with foil and leave to rest for 5 minutes.

4. Add the mustard and gherkins to the sauce, and simmer very gently for 5 minutes.

5. Serve the chops with a spoonful of sauce on top, and mash on the side.

Delicious with... a good red Beaujolais, like a Morgon, from the south of Burgundy.

Serves 4
5 mins preparation
25 mins cooking

Faux-filet Béarnaise

Sirloin with Béarnaise Sauce

Ingredients

2 shallots, finely chopped
60ml white wine
30ml white wine vinegar
2 fresh tarragon sprigs,
finely chopped
Sea salt and milled black pepper
200g butter, cut into chunks
3 medium egg yolks
4 x 2cm thick aged sirloin steaks
2 teaspoons vegetable oil

To serve
Watercress
Shop-bought good quality crisps

Equipment
Electric hand mixer

Follow my method for a classic Béarnaise sauce, and you'll be delighted with the results – the secret is to keep the eggs foamy and not overcook them. The sauce can accompany any cut of beef, including a roast. With this sirloin, watercress and homemade crisps are a traditional garnish, but you can cheat by reheating good quality shop-bought crisps in the oven.

1. Place the shallots, wine, vinegar, tarragon and seasoning in a medium-size saucepan. Simmer slowly for 10 minutes until just one tablespoon of liquid remains.

2. When the shallots have cooked for 5 minutes, place the butter in a second saucepan and heat on medium until melted and hot. Discard the whitish foam from the surface and transfer the butter to a jug for easy pouring.

3. Over a very low heat, add the egg yolks to the shallot and wine reduction, and start whisking immediately with an electric hand mixer. After 10 seconds, turn off the heat. The egg should be slightly cooked and foamy, but not scrambled. Still whisking, gradually add the warm butter, very slowly, pouring it in a thin trickle. Stop before you get to the white residue that lies at the bottom of the jug. Cover the pan and keep it warm near the stove, while you cook the steaks. A Béarnaise cannot be reheated.

4. Heat a large pan on high. Season the steaks well, then brush lightly with oil. When your pan is smoking hot, reduce the heat to medium, add the steaks and cook for 4 minutes, flipping them every minute, for rare. One more minute on each side will give you medium rare.

5. Serve with a spoonful of Béarnaise, watercress and crisps.

   Tip: Use the stopwatch on your phone for perfect timing.

The ideal wine for this dish... a red Bordeaux, such as a Fronsac from the Aquitaine region.

Carré d'Agneau Crème à l'Ail

Rack of Lamb with Garlic Cream

Ingredients

2 x 6-chop racks of lamb
Sea salt and milled black pepper
4 fresh rosemary sprigs, chopped
10 garlic cloves
20g butter
1 teaspoon sugar
¼ teaspoon sea salt
350ml double cream

To serve

Ratatouille
(see page 72 for my recipe)

Equipment

Freezer bag
Electric hand blender (optional)

To select the best lamb, look for deep pink flesh and white fat. The French love garlic with lamb, and often stud the leg or rack with garlic cloves before cooking. I prefer to serve it with this very special garlic sauce, where the flavours are softened by cooking the garlic with sugar. You can easily halve this recipe to serve two.

1. Pre-heat the oven to 220°C/fan 200°C/gas mark 7. Line a baking tray with kitchen foil.

2. Season the lamb racks and pan-fry, fat side down, for 3 minutes. Transfer to the baking tray, fat side up. Sprinkle rosemary over the top and underneath each rack. Bake for 22 minutes for medium rare. If you like it more cooked, give it a few more minutes.

3. Meanwhile, to peel and mash the garlic quickly, place the cloves in a freezer bag and bash lightly with a rolling pin. Open the bag and remove the skin from the cloves, which will come off easily. Cut the cloves in half and discard any bitter green centre. Close the bag again, and continue bashing with the rolling pin until all the garlic is mashed.

4. Place the garlic, butter, sugar and salt in a small saucepan, and simmer gently for 10 minutes. Add the cream and simmer for 10 more minutes. Pass the sauce through a sieve and keep until you're ready to serve, or you can blend it with an electric hand blender for a more intense garlic flavour.

5. Take the racks out of the oven, cover with kitchen foil and leave to rest while you set the table. Carve and serve with the garlic sauce and ratatouille.

Tip: You can cook the ratatouille in advance and reheat it gently while the lamb is cooking – it tastes even better the day after you've made it.

Perfect with... a red Bordeaux, like a Pauillac from the Haut-Medoc.

Les plats / Main courses - Vegetarian

When you're cooking for vegetarians or simply fancy a change from meat, there are all sorts of delicious options open to you. These recipes are truly tasty and satisfying, packed with authentic French flavour.

Pavés de Tofu aux Deux Poivres, Sauce Crémée aux Cèpes

Pepper-Coated Tofu with Creamy Porcini Sauce

Ingredients

20 dried cèpes or porcini mushrooms
1½ tablespoons green peppercorns
2 teaspoons pink peppercorns
2 tablespoons fresh chives, chopped
½ teaspoon sea salt flakes
500g tofu
1 tablespoon Dijon mustard
40g butter, melted
50g shallots, finely chopped
Sea salt to season
2 tablespoons Cognac or whisky
1 bay leaf
2 tablespoons crème fraîche
2 teaspoons cornflour

To serve

Buttered green beans
(see page 68 for my recipe)

Equipment

Baking parchment

For pepper lovers, this is a vegetarian take on 'steak au poivre', with an aromatic, creamy mushroom sauce. It's important to use a good quality French crème fraîche, such as d'Isigny – you'll find this gives the sauce a nice, smooth texture.

1. Soak the mushrooms in 400ml of hot water for 10 minutes.

2. Pre-heat the oven to 210°C/fan 190°C/gas mark 6½. Line a baking tray with baking parchment.

3. Place the green and pink peppercorns on a chopping board, and chop finely with a knife. Mix with the chives and salt flakes.

4. Cut the tofu into 4 thick chunks, and dry well on kitchen paper. Slice one chunk in half horizontally, open and spread the inside with ½ teaspoon of mustard. Close, brush the top with melted butter and sprinkle with ¼ of the peppercorn mixture. Repeat with the other chunks.

5. Transfer the prepared tofu to the lined baking tray and bake for 15 minutes.

6. Meanwhile in a medium-size frying pan, fry the shallots in butter over a high heat for 5 minutes, until nicely caramelised. Season well, add the Cognac or whisky, and let it boil down for 30 seconds. Add the mushrooms, soaking liquid and bay leaf. Simmer for 10 minutes.

7. Mix the remaining mustard with the crème fraîche and cornflour, until well blended. Add this mixture to the sauce and stir. Let it simmer for a couple of minutes, until the sauce thickens.

8. Take the tofu out of the oven and serve with the mushroom sauce and green beans.

Try this with... a red Macon from southern Burgundy.

Omelette Façon Mère Poulard

Soufflé Omelette

6 eggs
1 good pinch sea salt
2 tablespoons crème fraîche
20g butter
60g gruyère cheese, grated

To serve

Green salad or ratatouille
(see page 72 for my recipe)

Equipment

Electric hand mixer
26cm ovenproof non-stick
frying pan

The most famous omelette in France comes from Mont St Michel in Normandy, and was prepared by Annette Poulard, also known as 'la Mère Poulard'. Inspired by her recipe, I beat the yolks and whites separately, and then combine them to create a wonderfully light omelette that tastes like a soufflé and cooks in a flash.

1. Pre-heat the grill to maximum.

2. Separate the eggs, putting the whites in one bowl and the yolks in another. Add the salt to the whites and beat with the electric hand mixer for 1½ minutes, until soft peaks form. Add the crème fraîche to the yolks and beat for 1 minute.

3. Heat the butter in the frying pan.

4. Fold a big spoonful of the whites into the yolks and stir gently, then fold this mixture back into the whites. Stir gently again, swirling and lifting to avoid breaking too many air bubbles.

5. Pour the egg mixture into the frying pan. Cook for 2 minutes, constantly but gently shaking the pan.

6. Sprinkle with the grated cheese and place under the grill (if the grill has a door, leave it open). Let the omelette cook for about a minute, until the cheese is just melted.

7. Carefully take the pan from the grill (the handle will be hot). Fold the omelette in two and transfer it to a serving plate. Cut in half and serve at once with a salad or ratatouille.

And to drink... choose a white Crémant de Bourgogne, a sparkling wine from Burgundy.

Les garnitures / Vegetable garnishes

If you've ever been to a French market, you'll know we have wonderful vegetables. We often prepare them quite simply to enhance the main dish – and this way, their quality really shines through. Discover classic potato dishes, including gratin dauphinois, and a clever way to enhance peas.

Gratin Dauphinois

Potato Gratin

300ml whole milk
150ml double cream
1 nutmeg
650g large Charlotte potatoes
5g soft butter
1 small garlic clove, crushed
Sea salt and milled black pepper
50g Gruyère cheese, grated
(optional)

30 x 20cm gratin dish

There are many recipes for this classic potato dish. Some use floury potatoes, some don't use cheese, and some use only cream and no milk. I've tried countless variations, and always come back to this one.

1. Pre-heat the grill to maximum.

2. Rinse a large pan with cold water, and don't dry it. Pour in the milk and cream, add about 8 gratings of nutmeg, and heat gently.

3. Meanwhile, peel the potatoes and slice very thinly. Add them to the milk pan as you go, then simmer for 15 minutes. They should be tender when you pierce them with a knife.

4. Mix the butter and garlic, and spread the mixture over the inside of the gratin dish. Spoon the potatoes and creamy milk into the dish and season.

5. If you're using the cheese, sprinkle it on top of the gratin before placing under the grill for 5 minutes, until the top is brown and bubbling. If you're not using the cheese, place the gratin straight under the grill to brown. Serve warm.

Purée de Pommes de Terre

Classic French Mashed Potatoes

Ingredients

1kg King Edward potatoes
About 200ml whole milk (quantity depends on potato variety)
½ teaspoon sea salt
100g butter, diced

Equipment

Steamer or steam basket
Potato ricer or potato masher

In 1980, the famous French chef, Joël Robuchon, came up with a mash recipe that literally made his reputation. It was so good, his customers would skip desserts for another helping! His extremely rich version uses 250g of butter for 1kg of potatoes – mine uses only 100g, but feel free to increase this if you're feeling indulgent.

1. Whether you're using a steamer or a steam basket over a pan of water, bring the water to a boil.

2. Meanwhile, peel the potatoes and cut into 4cm cubes. Place in the steamer or basket, and cook for 15 minutes.

3. Warm up the milk in a saucepan.

4. In another saucepan, mash the potatoes or put them through a ricer. Add the salt, and place the pan over a low heat for 2 minutes to dry the mixture.

5. Add the butter and stir until melted and blended.

6. Add about 100ml of warm milk, whisk the mash until soft and smooth, then add more milk if needed. Check the seasoning and serve at once.

Légumes Verts au Beurre

Buttered Green Vegetables

Ingredients

1 tablespoon coarse sea salt
500ml ice cubes
600g green beans, trimmed
10g butter
Sea salt and milled black pepper
or
1kg long-leaf spinach,
trimmed and washed
10g butter
or
1 Savoy cabbage (about 900g)
halved, cored and thinly sliced
50g butter

The French technique for cooking green beans, spinach or cabbage is the same: blanching in boiling water followed by a quick plunge in iced cold water to stop the cooking process. This keeps the vegetables nice and green, and you simply reheat them just before you want to serve them.

1. Pour 3 litres of boiling water from the kettle into a large pan (do this in 2 batches) and bring it back to the boil. Add the salt and let it dissolve for 15 seconds.

2. Meanwhile, place the ice cubes in a large bowl and cover with 2 litres of cold water.

3. Cook the green beans for 5 minutes, drain them in the colander and drop them in the iced water. Leave for 30 seconds, then drain again and dry on kitchen paper.

4. Just before serving, heat the butter in a large frying pan, add the beans and cook for 3 minutes until warm, tossing occasionally. Check the seasoning and serve.

For the spinach
Follow the same method as for the green beans, but blanch the spinach for only 1 minute and reheat with butter for 2 minutes.

For the cabbage
Follow the same method as for the green beans, but blanch the cabbage for 3 minutes. Reheat with 30g of the butter for 10 minutes, adding the remaining 20g 1 minute before the end.

Tip: If you use baby spinach, it's best to miss out the blanching and cook it directly in the frying pan for a couple of minutes, and then add the 10g of butter half way through cooking.

Serves 4
10 mins preparation
15 mins cooking

Petits Pois à la Française

French-style Peas

Ingredients

600g frozen peas
70g unsmoked bacon,
finely chopped
20g butter
1 onion, finely chopped
2 small gem lettuces,
each cut into 6 lengthways
2 fresh thyme sprigs
½ teaspoon sugar
150ml ready-made fresh
chicken stock
Sea salt and milled black pepper

Equipment
Sauté pan or heavy pot with a lid

I've used frozen peas in this recipe for two reasons. They're much more convenient than fresh and (unless the fresh peas have just been picked) they taste much better.

1. Place the peas in a bowl and cover with boiling water from the kettle. Leave for 5 minutes.

2. In the sauté pan or pot, cook the bacon in butter for 3 minutes. Add the onion and cook for 2 minutes, until it's soft and the bacon is crisp.

3. Add the lettuce and thyme, and cook for 30 seconds.

4. Drain the peas and add them to the pan with the sugar and stock. Bring to a simmer and cook for 5 minutes. Check the seasoning, turn off the heat and cover. Let the peas sit for a couple of minutes before serving.

   Tip: For vegetarians, leave out the bacon, and cook the onions for 5 minutes, until slightly caramelised. Use three gem lettuces instead of two, and vegetable stock instead of chicken.

Ratatouille

Serves 4
10 mins preparation
20 mins cooking

Vegetable Stew

Ingredients

6 tablespoons olive oil
2 onions, cut into thin wedges
2 garlic cloves, crushed
500g tomatoes, halved,
deseeded and chopped
3 fresh thyme sprigs
1 teaspoon sugar
1 large aubergine,
cut into 3cm chunks
Sea salt to season
2 courgettes, halved and
finely sliced
1 red pepper, halved,
deseeded and finely sliced
1 green pepper, halved,
deseeded and finely sliced
1 tablespoon red wine vinegar

Equipment

2-litre heavy casserole pot with a lid
(suitable for using on a hob)

In many French ratatouille recipes, you stir-fry all the vegetables separately and mingle them at the end. This version is much faster, as you cook all the vegetables at the same time – yet it still looks and tastes fantastic.

1. Pre-heat the grill to maximum.

2. Line the oven tray with foil.

3. Heat 2 tablespoons of oil in the casserole pot. Fry the onions over a high heat for 5 minutes, until tender and slightly brown around the edges.

4. Add the garlic, tomatoes, thyme and sugar to the onions, and simmer for 20 minutes.

5. Meanwhile, heat 2 tablespoons of oil in a large frying pan. Add the aubergine chunks and cook for 15 minutes, stirring occasionally until golden. Season with salt half-way through.

6. While the aubergines are cooking, arrange the courgette slices on one half of the oven tray and the red and green pepper slices on the other. Season, brush with oil, and cook under the grill – as close as possible – for 15 minutes until softened.

7. Stir the aubergine, courgettes and peppers into the onion and tomato mixture. Add the vinegar, check the seasoning and mix delicately.

8. Cover and leave to infuse for a few minutes while you get the rest of the meal ready.

   Tip: You can prepare the ratatouille in advance, and eat it warm or cold. It's delicious served with a poached egg (see page 14 for my recipe).

Les desserts et petit fours /
Desserts and confectionery

Desserts are the most important part of the meal in France, and often evoke childhood memories. Many French desserts are quicker and easier to prepare than they look, and I've collected some of my favourites here – including a special treat: my grandmother's irresistibly gooey chocolate cake.

Crêpes Suzette

Flambé Crepes in Orange and Grand-Marnier Sauce

Ingredients

150g plain flour
30g caster sugar
¼ teaspoon sea salt
2 eggs plus 1 yolk
350ml whole milk
80g butter, melted
40g caster sugar
60ml Grand Marnier
100ml freshly
squeezed orange juice

The story goes that an apprentice at the Café de Paris in Monaco in the late 1800s spilt alcohol on a pile of crepes – then he reheated them and they caught fire. He served them anyway and the customer, the future King Edward VII, loved the flambé taste. He asked for them to be named after his companion, Suzette.

1. Mix the flour, 30g of sugar and salt in a bowl. Make a well in the centre and add the eggs and yolk. Whisk the eggs, gradually pulling in the flour and slowly adding half of the milk. When the batter is smooth, add the remaining milk and 2 tablespoons of melted butter, and whisk again.

2. Heat the frying pan. Butter the surface with a piece of kitchen paper dipped in melted butter. Pour a small ladle of batter (about 75ml) into the middle of the pan and immediately swirl the pan to thinly coat the bottom. Cook until golden – probably for less than a minute.

3. Flip the crepe over using a spatula and cook for another minute. Place on a warm plate and keep covered with a clean tea towel. Repeat to make 10 crepes. At least 8 of them should turn out well – fold these into quarters.

4. To finish, heat half of the remaining butter in the frying pan. Sprinkle with 20g of sugar and leave for a minute until the sugar is melted and caramelised. Add 4 crepes and 2 tablespoons of Grand Marnier. Tip the pan towards the gas flame to ignite the alcohol. Be careful: the flames might be tall. Shake the pan until the flames disappear, then add 50ml of the orange juice and leave to bubble for 30 seconds. Divide the crepes and sauce between 2 warm plates. Repeat for the last 4 crepes. Serve at once.

Tip: If you don't have a gas cooker, after adding the Grand Marnier, light with a match – but do be careful, the flames can be quite tall!

And to drink... a late harvest Muscat from Alsace goes beautifully with the orangey flavours.

Poires Pochées Vin et Groseille

Pears in Red Wine and Redcurrant Syrup

Ingredients

1 orange
1 lemon
1 bottle Beaujolais
300g redcurrant jelly
1 large cinnamon stick
10 black peppercorns
4 ripe pears

To serve

Almond biscuits

You can poach these pears in any wine, but I particularly like them in Beaujolais – as in the original regional recipe. This is the perfect dessert for a winter meal, and any leftover liquid is lovely in white wine or champagne.

1. Using a vegetable peeler, cut 2 long (10cm) strips of zest from the orange and 2 from the lemon. (Reserve the fruit for other recipes).

2. Place the wine, jelly, orange and lemon zest, cinnamon and peppercorns in the saucepan. Bring to a simmer and cook for a few minutes to dissolve the jelly.

3. Peel the pears with a vegetable peeler, keeping the stems intact. As you finish peeling each one, place it in the simmering wine mixture. Simmer the pears for 12-15 minutes. Check they're tender all the way through by piercing with a knife.

4. Ladle all the poaching liquid into a large frying pan (where it will evaporate faster) and boil for 10 minutes, until the volume is reduced by half and the texture becomes syrupy. Pour this back over the pears and leave to cool.

5. Serve the pears lukewarm or cold, drizzled with the syrup. Almond biscuits go nicely with them.

Tip: The golden rule for cooking with wine is, "do not cook with a wine you would not drink". Make sure the Beaujolais tastes good before you use it!

And to drink with this... try the same wine we use in the recipe – Beaujolais.

Gâteau au Chocolat de Grand-Mère

Grandmother's Chocolate Cake

Ingredients

200g good quality
cooking chocolate
150g unsalted butter,
plus extra for greasing
½ teaspoon sea salt
35g ground almonds
15g cornflour
4 medium eggs
120g caster sugar

To Serve
Icing sugar

Equipment
23cm round cake tin
Baking parchment
Electric hand mixer

Like a cross between a pie and a cake, this gluten-free dessert is wonderfully light and moist. As kids, we used to eat it still warm, straight out of the tin with a spoon – which drove my grandmother mad. If you can resist, it's even better the following day.

1. To save time, make sure you have all the ingredients and equipment to hand.

2. Pre-heat the oven to 210°C/fan 190°C/gas mark 6½.

3. Pour about 300ml of hot water from the kettle into a medium-size saucepan and place over a low heat.

4. Chop the chocolate and butter into small pieces and place in a large bowl. Add the salt and place the bowl over the pan of simmering water. Make sure the bottom of the bowl doesn't touch the water, so the chocolate doesn't overheat and curdle. Stir occasionally.

5. Meanwhile, butter the cake tin and line with a square of baking parchment. Press the parchment gently against the edges, keeping the ripples in it, which will give a flower shape to the cake. Trim any excess paper off the top.

6. In a separate bowl, mix the almonds and cornflour until well blended.

7. Stir the chocolate and take it off the heat, even if some bits are not melted.

8. Whisk the eggs and sugar for 2 minutes with the hand mixer, until double in size and light in colour.

9. By now, the chocolate and butter will be completely melted and no warmer than body temperature. Stir the mixture until smooth.

10. With a large spatula, stir the egg mixture into the chocolate, working quickly. Then gently fold in the ground almonds and cornflour by swirling and lifting the batter.

11. Pour the mixture into the lined tin. Tap the bottom on the worktop 4 times to bring up and pop any bubbles, and bake for 18 minutes. The centre should be soft but not wobbly

12. Serve warm or cold, dusted with icing sugar.

Tip: for the best results, use the fan oven setting.

Drink suggestion... a sweet red Rivesaltes from the Languedoc-Roussillon would be perfect.

Tarte Fine aux Pommes

Thin Apple Tart

Ingredients

320g pack ready rolled
all butter puff pastry
2 large Golden Delicious apples
2 tablespoons apricot jam
30g butter, melted
3 tablespoons icing sugar

To serve
Crème fraiche

Equipment
Baking parchment
Apple corer
Pastry brush
Tea strainer or fine sieve

With very finely cut apples, coated with butter and sugar several times during baking, this classic tart really melts in the mouth.

1. Pre-heat the oven to 220°C/fan 200°C/gas mark 7. Line a baking tray with baking parchment.

2. Unroll the pastry. Using a 23cm plate as a guide, cut out a circle of pastry and place it on the lined baking tray. Keep the leftover pastry.

3. Prick the pastry base all over with a fork; this will prevent it from shrinking.

4. Core and peel the apples. Cut them in half lengthways, then cut each half into very thin slices (about 3mm).

5. Spread the apricot jam over the circle of pastry. Arrange the apple slices over the top, overlapping them slightly, in 2 concentric rings to make the shape of a flower. Brush with melted butter and, using a tea strainer or fine sieve, dust generously with about 1 tablespoon of icing sugar.

6. Bake for 10 minutes, then remove from the oven, brush with butter again and dust with more icing sugar. Return to the oven for 5 more minutes, then repeat with the butter and sugar. Cook for a final 5 minutes until the tart is nicely caramelised on top. Serve lukewarm with a scoop of crème fraiche.

Tip: For best results and a crispier base, use the conventional oven setting.

And to drink... try a sweet, aromatic Chenin Blanc from the Loire Valley.

Gâteau Roulé au Citron

Baked Lemon Curd and Cream Roly-Poly

Ingredients

4 egg whites
1 pinch fine sea salt
90g caster sugar
6 egg yolks
25g plain flour
25g cornflour
300ml whipping cream
2 tablespoons icing sugar
Grated zest and juice of 1 lemon
1 teaspoon honey
350g good quality lemon curd

To serve

Icing sugar

Equipment

Electric hand mixer
2 sheets baking parchment,
30 x 40cm

Every country has a roly-poly recipe. The French one is made with a light sponge that bakes in no time – and the choice of fillings is endless. Here we use lemon curd, but you could also use jam, chocolate hazelnut spread, chestnut cream or fruit compote.

1. Pre-heat the oven to 220°C/fan 200°/gas mark 7. Line a baking tray with one of the sheets of parchment.

2. Beat the egg whites with a pinch of salt until they form soft peaks. With the beaters still running, slowly add 40g of the sugar. When the whites are glossy and stiff, beat for 20 seconds more and then put to one side.

3. Add the remaining 50g of sugar to the egg yolks and beat for exactly 2 minutes, until foamy and light in colour.

4. Carefully fold the yolk mixture into the beaten whites in 2 batches, swirling and lifting gently to avoid breaking the air bubbles.

5. Add the flour and cornflour in the same way.

6. Pour the batter onto the lined baking tray and spread delicately into a 25 x 35cm rectangle. Bake for 8 minutes until puffed and golden.

7. Remove the sponge from the oven, lift it by the paper and place on a rack. Cover with a clean tea towel to cool.

8. Meanwhile, whip the cream, icing sugar and grated zest of half the lemon – until not quite, but almost, stiff.

9. Squeeze the lemon and mix the juice with the honey.

10. Flip the cake over onto the second sheet of baking parchment. Peel the paper off the upturned base by rolling it close to the cake surface rather than lifting it; this avoids damaging the sponge.

11. Drizzle the sponge with the lemon juice and honey mixture. Spread a layer of lemon curd over the surface, followed by a layer of the whipped cream mixture, leaving a 2cm gap around the edges.

12. Roll the sponge tightly from the short end, lifting the paper to help the rolling. Transfer it to a serving plate and leave to cool in the fridge. Serve sliced with a dusting of icing sugar..

And to drink with this... a sweet white Muscat de Rivesaltes from the Languedoc-Roussillon will go very nicely.

Serves 10
5 mins preparation
10 mins soaking

Pruneaux Rhum Vanille

Rum and Vanilla Macerated Prunes

Ingredients

500g stoned soft prunes
2 Darjeeling tea bags
½ vanilla pod
300g honey
300ml rum

Equipment

1-litre preserving jar, sterilised

You can make a substantial amount of these sweet, boozy prunes, as they keep in the fridge for a month. Then you have them as the perfect stand-by dessert for an impromptu dinner. Serve them with ice cream or grandmother's chocolate cake – or simply with coffee after the meal.

1. Sterilise the preserving jar by submerging in boiling water for 2 minutes. Take it out and dry. Alternatively, run it through your dishwasher on a full cycle.

2. Place the prunes in a bowl with the tea bags and cover with boiling water.

3. Leave for 3 minutes, then remove the tea bags. Let the prunes soak for 7 more minutes.

4. Meanwhile, split the vanilla pod open and scrape out the seeds. Mix the vanilla pod, seeds and honey in a saucepan, and heat gently until the honey becomes liquid. Don't let it boil – this is just to warm up the vanilla to help the flavours develop.

5. Add the rum and mix well.

6. Drain the prunes, add them to the honey-rum mixture and stir gently. Place in the preserving jar.

7. You can eat the prunes straight away – or keep them in the fridge for up to a month, letting them become tastier and tastier.

Truffes au Chocolat

Chocolate Truffles

Ingredients

130g good quality dark chocolate
A large pinch of sea salt
25g cold butter, cut into
small pieces
2 tablespoons
chocolate hazelnut spread
1 tablespoon crème fraiche
1 tablespoon cocoa powder

Equipment

Small stainless steel bowl
Piping bag or small freezer bag
Mini paper cases (optional)

During the Christmas of 1895, chocolatier Louis Dufour ran out of chocolate. Not wanting to lose face, he decided to mix cream and cocoa butter into a 'ganache', and roll this in cocoa powder. It was an instant success; chocolate truffles were born. Still very popular today, this is a fun and easy recipe.

1. Chop the chocolate into thin pieces and place in a small stainless steel bowl with the salt.

2. Set the bowl over a small pan of simmering water, making sure the bottom doesn't touch the water. Stir occasionally.

3. After 3-4 minutes, remove from the heat and stir well, making sure all the chocolate is melted.

4. Add the butter, stirring until it melts and the mixture becomes glossy.

5. Add the chocolate hazelnut spread and crème fraîche. By now, the mixture will have thickened.

6. Spoon the mixture into a piping bag (you can make your own by cutting the corner off a small freezer bag). Squeeze out the truffles, about the size of a big cherry, onto a plate.

7. Leave to cool in the fridge for 5 minutes.

8. Spread the cocoa on a plate and roll each truffle in it, until well coated.

9. Place the truffles in paper cases or on a serving plate. Keep in a cool place until you're ready to serve.

Try these with... a cup of very good coffee, or a Calvados or Cognac.

Rocher-Coco

Coconut Macaroons

Ingredients

2 egg whites
90g caster sugar
150g desiccated coconut

Equipment

Baking parchment

Named after their rock-like character, these little bites come from the French Antilles in the Caribbean. High-temperature baking makes them crispy outside and deliciously moist inside – a wonderful way to use leftover egg whites.

1. Pre-heat the oven to 220°C/fan 200°C/gas mark 7. Line a baking tray with baking parchment.

2. Place all the ingredients in a medium-size saucepan and mix well. Cook over a very low heat for 3 minutes, until the mixture becomes sticky but no more than slightly hot to the touch. Transfer to a bowl and leave to cool for 2 minutes.

3. When still warm but cool enough to handle, squeeze a tablespoon of the mixture in your palm to form a small ball with a slight point. Repeat to make 12 macaroons, placing them on the lined baking tray.

4. Bake for 10 minutes, until dark brown on the outside.

Enjoy these with... a sweet Muscat from Alsace.

Apéritifs et amuse-bouches /
Drinks and nibbles

Amuse-bouches is probably my favourite phrase in culinary French. What better way to start a meal than by amusing your taste buds? Give your guests something delicious to nibble on, while you put the finishing touches to your meal. Best of all, these recipes are very simple, and fun to prepare.

Kir Royal

Ingredients

1 teaspoon Crème de Cassis
180ml Champagne, chilled

Equipment

Champagne flutes

Every region in France has developed its own version of Kir – wine or cider with Crème de Cassis. For example, a Kir Breton is made with dry cider, and a Kir Alsacien with sparkling Crémant d' Alsace. Kir Royal is the luxury version! This recipe is a rough guideline; feel free to adjust the amount of Crème de Cassis according to your taste.

1. Pour the Crème de Cassis into a Champagne flute.
2. Top up with Champagne and serve.

    Tips:

    To open a bottle of Champagne safely, hold the bottle at a 45° angle, away from your guests. Remove the foil top and wire cage. Grip the cork firmly and twist the bottle very slowly to release the cork, keeping the bottle at the same angle to let the pressure escape.

    To chill Champagne quickly, add a big handful of rock salt to the ice in your ice bucket. The salt melts the ice and the temperature drops sharply.

Mimosa

Ingredients

100ml freshly
squeezed orange juice
1½ teaspoons Cointreau
60ml Champagne, chilled
Orange slices to garnish

Equipment

Champagne flutes

The French lay claim to this cocktail, created in 1925 at the Ritz in Paris. But really it's a take on the Buck's Fizz, invented four years earlier in London at the Buck's Club.

1. Pour the orange juice and Cointreau into a Champagne flute.

2. Hold the glass at an angle and slowly pour in the Champagne. The mixture will froth, so fill the glass half way and wait for a few seconds before topping up with more Champagne.

3. Decorate with a slice of orange and serve.

   Tip: Don't waste your best Champagne on cocktails; use a non-vintage or a 'crémant' from Alsace, Burgundy or the Loire.

Serves 1
5 mins preparation

Dubonnet Faux Martini

Fortified Wine Cocktail

Ingredients

1 orange
Ice cubes
100ml Dubonnet
1 tablespoon Noilly Prat
¼ teaspoon Cointreau

Equipment

Cocktail sticks
Martini glass

Dubonnet is a blend of fortified wine, herbs and spices. You can enjoy it on its own or use it in cocktails. This one, with a little Noilly Prat and Cointreau, makes the perfect dinner party aperitif.

1. Wash and brush the orange under hot water, then use a vegetable peeler to remove some long strands of peel. Thread these on a cocktail stick and keep to one side.

2. Place about 8 ice cubes in a 500ml jug. Add the Dubonnet, Noilly Prat and Cointreau. Stir well.

3. Strain into a martini glass and decorate with the orange peel.

Thé Glacé Camomille-Clémentine

Camomile and Clementine Iced Tea

Ingredients

6 clementines
6 camomile tea bags
Ice cubes
500ml lemonade

Equipment

1-litre jug
Tumbler glasses

Unique and non-alcoholic, this refreshing, herbal version of iced tea is perfect for hot summer evenings.

1. Wash and brush the clementines under hot water, and cut 3 of them into slices.

2. Place the camomile tea bags and sliced clementines in a heatproof 1-litre jug. Add 700ml of boiling water from the kettle and leave for 15 minutes.

3. Remove the tea bags and add 500ml of ice cubes. This will cool the mixture rapidly.

4. Slice 2 of the remaining clementines and halve the last one.

5. Pour 200ml of the tea into a tumbler, then add a squeeze of juice from the halved clementine and 100ml of lemonade. Garnish with ice cubes and clementine slices and serve. Repeat for 4-5 servings.

Tapenade à l'Aubergine

Olive Paste with Aubergines

Ingredients

1 aubergine (300g), diced
2 tablespoons olive oil
250g good quality pitted black olives
50g capers, rinsed and drained
4 anchovy fillets in olive oil, drained
Grated zest and juice of ½ lemon
50ml extra virgin olive oil

To serve

Crusty baguette
20 radishes

Equipment

Food processor

Tapenade comes from the Provencal word 'tapenado', which means caper sauce – but it's really an olive paste. The quality of the olives you use makes a big difference to the end result. I like to use the small Niçoise ones but Kalamata also work well. Adding aubergine is a trick I use to cut the saltiness and give the tapenade a smooth texture.

1. Pan-fry the aubergine in 2 tablespoons of olive oil, over high heat for 15 minutes, until it's well caramelised.

2. Meanwhile, slice the baguette and clean the radishes.

3. When the aubergine's done, place it on a large plate and leave to cool for a few minutes.

4. While the aubergine is cooling, place the olives, capers, anchovies and lemon zest in the food processor. Pulse a few times until finely shredded. Add the aubergine, lemon juice and extra virgin olive oil, and pulse a little longer until blended. Place in a serving bowl.

5. Serve the tapenade with the baguette slices and radishes on the side. Let your guests spread the tapenade on the bread, as thickly as they like!

   Tip: If you want a vegetarian alternative, this tapenade is also delicious without the anchovies.

Endives au Roquefort et Noix Caramelisées

Chicory with Roquefort and Caramelised Walnuts

Ingredients

15g butter
1 tablespoon caster sugar
¼ teaspoon sea salt
80g walnuts
150g Roquefort cheese
150g fromage frais, drained
1½ tablespoons fresh chives,
finely chopped
Milled black pepper
2 medium heads of chicory

Chicory, Roquefort and walnut is a classic salad combination in France. Here, everything's contained in the handy chicory leaves and the walnuts are crispy, sweet and salty – dangerously addictive! You can also serve these wicked walnuts as a nibble on their own.

1. Melt the butter in a medium frying pan. Add the sugar and salt, and cook for a minute on high, until the sugar starts to caramelise.

2. Add the walnuts, stirring to coat with the sugar, salt and butter. Reduce the heat to medium and cook for 2-3 minutes, stirring all the time, until well caramelised.

3. In a bowl, mix the Roquefort, fromage frais and chives roughly together – you want to end up with a lumpy mixture. Season with black pepper.

4. Trim and core the bottom of each chicory, and separate into 12 leaves. Wash the leaves and dry them well on kitchen paper.

5. Fill each leaf with a heaped tablespoon of the Roquefort mixture, and top with a couple of caramelised walnuts. Arrange on a serving plate.

Tip: For a chicory, Roquefort and walnut salad, arrange the chicory leaves and Roquefort on plates, then drizzle with the vinaigrette on page 14 and top with caramelised walnuts and chopped chives.

Serves 4 (16 rolls)
10 mins preparation
5 mins griling

Rouleaux de Pruneaux au Chèvre et Jambon Cru

Prune, Goats' Cheese and Cured Ham Rolls

Ingredients

80g firm goats' cheese with rind
8 large, ready-to-eat
pitted prunes, halved
8 slices of French cured
ham (Jambon de Bayonne)

Equipment

Cocktail sticks

Inspired by the classic prunes wrapped in bacon ('Devils on horseback'), these little morsels use goats' cheese and cured ham for a lighter, modern taste. You can prepare them in advance and grill them at the last minute – and if you can't find Jambon de Bayonne, Spanish Serrano ham also works well.

1. Pre-heat the grill to maximum. Line a baking tray with kitchen foil.

2. Place 1 teaspoon of goats' cheese in the centre of each half prune.

3. Cut a slice of cured ham in half lengthways. Lay one strip on the chopping board, place a stuffed halved prune at one end and roll, wrapping the ham tightly around the prune. Repeat for the rest of the ham, cheese and prunes.

4. Arrange the rolls on the lined baking tray, making sure the cheese side is facing upwards. Place under the grill for 5 minutes, until the ham is starting to brown and the cheese is slightly melted. Place on a serving plate with cocktail sticks for picking them up.

Tip: It's fashionable in France to invite your friends to an 'apéritif dinatoire', an all-aperitif dinner. If you'd like to try this yourself, serve these rolls along with the tapenade from page 102, and the cured salmon and cucumber tartare, chicken liver mousse and baked mushrooms with garlic butter from the starter chapter – and finish with coffee and the chocolate truffles from page 88.

Serves 4 (12 twists)

10 mins preparation
10 mins baking

Torsades au Fromage

Cheese Twists

Ingredients

1 egg
1 pinch sea salt
60g Gruyère cheese
320g pack ready rolled
all butter puff pastry
1½ tablespoons Dijon mustard
1 nutmeg
Milled black pepper

Equipment

Baking parchment
Pastry brush

Cheese twists are always a favourite to nibble with drinks – and so much nicer when they're freshly baked. In this recipe, I've pepped them up with a touch of mustard and grated nutmeg.

1. Pre-heat the oven to 220°C/fan 200°C/gas mark 7. Line a baking tray with baking parchment.

2. Whisk the egg lightly with a good pinch of salt. Finely grate the cheese.

3. Unroll the puff pastry on the work surface. Cut in half, keeping one half in the fridge for another recipe. Brush the half you're using with egg, and spread with mustard.

4. Sprinkle the cheese evenly over the top, pressing it down, so it sticks to the surface. Grate nutmeg generously over the cheese, and season with freshly milled black pepper.

5. Cut the pastry into twelve 1.5cm strips, along the shorter side.

6. Lift a strip, twist it, then transfer it to the lined baking tray. Press both ends lightly into the parchment to help the twist hold its shape.

7. Repeat, until you have 12 strips arranged on the baking tray. Brush any bare pastry (the bits without cheese) with egg and bake for 9-10 minutes, until well puffed and golden. Serve warm or cold.

Tip: You can also bake these untwisted, as flat cheese straws.

About Howdens Joinery

Howdens Joinery is the UK's largest manufacturer and supplier of fitted kitchens, appliances and joinery products. We understand what it takes to make a great looking kitchen, and importantly one that works every time, every day. That's why we only sell our products directly to professional tradespeople like your local builder.

Our offer includes over 40 different kitchen designs, plus a range of accessories, worktops, doors, flooring, and a wide variety of Lamona appliances, sinks and taps, exclusive to Howdens. Lamona products are manufactured to the highest standards to ensure they are durable and reliable, and all Lamona appliances come with a 2 year manufacturer's guarantee.

Established in 1995, last year we supplied over 350,000 kitchens, 650,000 appliances and 550,000 sinks and taps to UK homes.

Our products are always in stock in each of our 590 depots throughout the UK, and in each depot trained designers are on hand to design your kitchen and support you and your builder throughout. Talk to your builder about Howdens and visit **www.howdens.com** to see our full range of kitchens and joinery products.

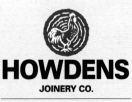

MAKING SPACE MORE VALUABLE

Exclusive to Howdens Joinery Co.

Bespoke Shelving Unit

Lamona White Ceramic Belfast Sink with Lamona Chrome Victorian Swan Neck Monobloc Tap

Timber Cutlery Tray

Lamona Professional 5 Burner Gas Hob

Lamona Built-Under Double Fan Oven

About the author

Food stylist and writer Valerie Berry was born in Paris, and spent much of her childhood helping her grandmother, who was obsessed with cooking. There she learned what life was really about: food.

These early experiences inspired Valerie to pursue many culinary adventures – such as starting her own catering business in the USA, running a pop-up restaurant in Paris, and working as a restaurant inspector for Egon Ronay's guides in London.

Today, Valerie is still based in London, but will never forget her French roots – as this book shows. Her other books include Basic Tapas (published in France and translated into five languages) and Soup!, published in the UK and Germany. She also contributes to The Guardian: Cook and is the author of New Vegetarian, a column in The Telegraph's Stella magazine.

Working on this book has been a delightful walk along memory lane for Valerie, and she is thrilled to share so many of the favourite recipes she grew up with.

www.valerieberry.com

Exclusive to Howdens Joinery Co.

www.lamona.co.uk